Poetically Seasoned

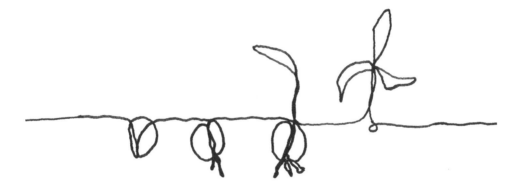

Debbie Chilton

TREATY OAK PUBLISHERS

Publisher's Note

Printed and published in the United States of America

Treaty Oak Publishers

ISBN-978-1-943658-79-4

Available in print and digital from Amazon

Back cover art: *Seedsons* by Debbie Chilton

DEDICATION

To my sons, Jake and Rusty.
I appreciate the way you live your life,
being true to yourself.

There have been a handful of books that I have read in wonder and this is one of them. The poems speak to a place deep within where inward reflection is a natural byproduct.

You'll love reading *Poetically Seasoned* to see where the journeys take you. I'm led to the place where I know I am nothing else but eternal love.

The collection is very engaging with a lovely flow and is easy to pick up again and again. It's timeless.

Kathryn K.

Debbie takes the threads of life and weaves a lyrical blanket. She never follows a pattern. Take the time to wrap yourself in the blanket and exhale.

Alistair D.

TABLE OF CONTENTS

Fall

RUMBLING

Rumbling into the night,
    Head mesmerized by thoughts of the day.
Contemplating quiet as a possibility.
    Aching for stillness and the solitude
        That awaits,
When Love slips inside the door.

WINDS OF CHANGE

Rustling the leaves
Stirring up the dust.
Let it take hold
    And carry you
        Into the next season of your life.
Riches are bountiful, here.
Changing the face of who you are.

TWISTED

Many things come and go
 Twirling, twisting, losing a piece into the turmoil
    Or triumph.
Tussled and intertwined
 Whirling, whizzing into the web of this world.
Gather up yourself, seek higher ground.
 You're safe there.
 It's what your core knows.
There is no danger, no life or death, desire to be everything.
Live in the essence called Love.

AN OPENING

Doors and windows
    Opening up to bring in
A breath of fresh air
    From the middle of Fall.
A chance of change begins when you look to see,
    A possibility beyond borders.
        Breathe in the coolness.
        Drink in what is to be.
God comes in, as bright as Light.
    And as quiet as the night.
Waiting for the chance for you
    To notice,
Her Presence.

TAKING FLIGHT

Taking Flight
When Love finds a way
    To love unconditionally,
        Many legacies fade away.
The passage of time exhibits itself
        like a breeze within the trees.
As if passing by, lifting leaves
Off into flight.

SPOT OF TIME

In the knowing,
    And not knowing, just the same.
The How, the Why, and the Where.
    The connecting point
Takes another spot of time,
    To realize an open portal awaits.

THE STAGE

Patterned players of life's day to day.
Scheduled practices
    And perfect performances is
One way to death
    Of your way called living.
Showing your need to judge
    Hoping to keep the fear of reality
From choking the voice
    From your throat.
Put down the sword
That resides in your mouth
    Sharply, shaped like a tongue.
For you are the first to get
    Cut when speaking.
Me thinks you protest too much.

ACTORS

The stage within
　　Where all the drama plays out.
Some take to the stage
　　Where all you see
Is the play
　　Called life.
Some hope to hell
For it all to stay inside
While others hope it to not be.
Everyone can see the mess they are inside.
The audience takes performers of all kinds
To see the actors, we all are.

THE DANCE FLOOR

Feeling separate and alone
    So far from home.
Pain reaching back to where
    Paths began.
Knowing still, that my
Dance
    Is surrounded in the
Never-ending swirl of love.
    My alone and truth
Speak a different language,
    Missing the beat.
Love patiently awaits, while getting her toes stepped on.
Holding the dancers frame
    Support glides along
    The dance floor, the best he can.
Awaiting the perfect step with his partner where they become one,
And separate is no more.

ANCHORED

Hanging on to that which is heavy
Like an anchor
    Secured in the deep.
Shortens your way
And lengthens the stay
    Of falling into the abyss of God's Pure Love.

SPEED BUMPS

The love of someone begins with
    Fully loving yourself
A clean, clear path
    Brightly lit.
Ease of connection
No ripples of thoughts
Existing as speed bumps
Slowing you down

SURRENDER

Letting go of all that I know.
Watching you leave
Knowing you are free.

Free with a price, a price that tears
Into the past.

Rich pain so deep
Leaving a legacy anew.

Hope…
Sits and waits, painfully quiet
For Love to prevail on the road beyond.

TENACITY

Treacherous treasures
Living on the edge.
Many worlds meet and find
A reflection like none other.

Carrying all of who you are far beyond
A reachable end.
Expansiveness explodes
Engaging the concubines of
The night.
Teasing disaster with tantalizing
Courage.

Ride on Brave One.
Your uncharted territory awaits.

SPEAKER OF THE HOUSE

Nestled under the layers of life,
    God Speaks

LET GO

Letting go
    Falling through
        In darkness
Or in light
A journey without a map
    What will you know in the end?
Will you survive?

DISSERVICE

Figuring it out, solving it
　　Fixing it for others.
All for what?
　　To distract you from your own pain?
Looks good.
Earns medals for some.
Yet when out of line, a possible disservice for all.

RELEASE

Shoes left behind
    Still looking as if they were
    Greeting each other.
An abandoned trail of clothes lay still
Revealing naked passion.
A slow and deliberate dance
    Maximizes the potential of Lust that fills the air.
Love expands as pleasure arises
    Riding the rhythmic waves of raw release
    That light up the darkened room
Cascading into grandeur explosions.

WARRIOR

Going to battle, loaded with your armor.
A familiar battlefield awaits your strategy
And earn yet another metal
    Collecting dust on your wall of honor.
How brave.

Shoes

Hope
Disaster
Hopeless Disaster.
Disastrously Hopeful.
Limitless possibilities to try on,
Like a new pair of shoes.

LETTING GO

Letting go, letting go and still holding on to more.
The letting go just keeps on coming.
Unpacking the bags for more to be revealed.
When is the letting go going to end?
Letting go of that one, too.

CAPTAIN AMERICA

Align yourself to all you are.
Touch points of your possible thoughts.
The moments that have come alive
And affected further than what has been known.
Go deep, hold on, thrust yourself
Beyond your thoughts or boundaries.
Exceed floating near your expectations.
For the world awaits the power
Of who you are!

MELANCHOLY

Here I sit
    In the quiet
    Feeling the movement of my breath
 Nourishing the body of my soul.
The beat of my heart
    Offers a cadence of music.
Searching for its rhythm, I wait.
And yet again when the world steps in to greet me,
    There is a glimmer of connection
    Forming a pattern to my path.
Secretly hidden only to be discovered
    By my noticing.
Consciously awake.
Awarding my intention with gratitude,
    In the quiet of solitude.

GOLDEN PRAIRIES IN FLIGHT

Golden light cascades down from the light blue sky displaying a warm glow against the fields.

The day sends showers into the distance at the base of the mountains.

Recently harvested fields shine bright in the sun. While some still glisten with snow.

The day is young. Inviting those curious to come along.

Translucent clouds play with the bright blue sky, dancing off into the distance.

Creating transforming art, in white.

Each golden blade of grass illuminates brighter, with hope for tomorrow.

Gleefully warmed by the bright sun of today.

The transition into Winter is slow and serene. Taking time to investigate its next move.

Quietly, the new day waits around the next bend.

BECAUSE

It's all because of you.
You are so giving.
Like caring for those who walk right in your front door.

Or, inspire those who hope to one day make a difference in giving
life or even saving a life.

Even still, you find more ways to give.
Your time.
Your knowledge.
And your heart.

Thank you for all that you do, all that you give,
All that you are.
Because of you, there is more to this world.

The Eye of The Storm

Sitting within the swirl of the storm
So easy to get lost in what flies by.
One concentrated distraction
Focused on what surrounds you,
Can sweep you off your feet.

Carrying you further from
The calm of the storm.

The eye,
A place to see all that is,
Clearly.
Where quiet can be found.
Allowing the present to exist.
Finding a connection to source, of inner strength,
A place where courage grows.
Supporting the next step
Into the stillness.

UPON US

Halloween is upon us.
    Or is it?
Or, has it been within us most recently?
Deciding undoubtedly,
    Especially when
        We can't say.
Did we already want or make the decision,
I Am Not
Who I was created to be?
        Even when
    Doubt enters into the room.
Or I decided, I did not matter.
This is My Halloween.

Night Collection

FULL MOON

"That little seductive touch will ignite a paradox of
spectacular events!!"
    Was the last message she read.
As she prepares for her lover
    She fiddles with her hair
    Moistens her lips
    Adjusts her shirt
Then, catches herself admiring her flirtatious smile in the
mirror,
    Lowering her head, she blushes and
Laughs out loud.
Is this possible?
    Yes, my Love, this is all for you…
This can be my life?
    Wait. This is my life!

SAVORING THE WAITING

More to come
    All that awaits her
 Is beyond
    Her limits.
May you be open to receive,
    And then…
 Savor in the waiting.

ANTICIPATION

The pronounced lover arrives,
Full of desire.
    A tremor
     Erupts
    As he knocks at the door, as gentle as his words.
Desire so deep of the expectant
History of escapades past.
Many thoughts conjure up
    All that she has to be,
To sit and to wait
    Full of Anticipation.

DESIRE

Many thoughts conjure up
    All that she has to be,
    To sit and to wait
    Full of anticipation.
Desire so deep of the expectant
    History of escapades past.
As he knocks at the door, as gentle as his words,
    A tremor
    Erupts
The pronounced lover arrives
    Full of Desire.

AFTERMATH

Sound asleep
Exhausted from a night of love,
He awakes
    Her with a brush of his lips
    On her cheek,
Whispering in her ear…
He is leaving again,
    In the middle of the night.
Leaving her waking for more disastrous yearning in the morning.
No one to seduce her but her dreams
    That explode with remembrance.
The night of desire has slipped into the day, dreaming.

EXPECTANCY

Many expectations that previous
Lovers arrived with, are not welcome here.
Only the savory juice of each
    Precious, present, moment.
Electrifying desire and delight
    Are so loudly proclaiming reverence beyond
    their estimation
 Of defined potential.

THANK YOU

To the love that she lost:
    Without room to explore,
There would be no discovery of things possible to come.
Many years of union creating gifts,
    To last a lifetime.
Thank you, my love
    For the Love that Lost.

Winter

CAMOUFLAGE

Standing on the edge.
Just me and my light.
Looking past all that's there, right in front of me.
Pretending it doesn't even exist.
Certainty says, it cannot be recognized, not in any form.
For what I cannot see, I do not even know.
The edge teeters on a path to nowhere, a path to everywhere.
One moment will decide.
Who will fall in first?
Me, or my light?

DISAPPOINTMENT

Expectations head into limits
Followed by disappointments,
Crashing down into the pain of self-pity.

Movement, breathe, life lives
 Only in a petri dish of openness.
Limitless, without boundaries are
 Available to so many
  Unforeseen experiences.
A place where your emotions cannot be your guide.
 They are there only to counsel.

THE GUARDIAN

Quietly, he sits
    Anxiously waiting his heart's desire.
To be loved like no other.
Scarred from Love's past,
    Cautiously awaiting
        A chance for something new.
For walls of stature and strength
    Guard all that he knows
Protecting his very existence.
Special permission has been granted.
    Allowing passage into his heart.
One moment in time, so preciously tender.

SOUNDS OF A GOODBYE

Whether spoken or felt.
It's like none other.
Heavy as an anchor,
    As freeing as flight.
You've been on both sides
    Every step of the way.
Each side of the coin, growing empathy.

PEOPLE POT

Meek and mild
    Tempered and hot.
Mixing together in
    A cast iron pot.
Steam rising as change takes place.
Adjoining together for one great taste.

SEARCHING

Mathematical anomalies
　　Searching for the answer
　　　　To all of life's questions.
Leaving many mesmerized in
　　A conundrum of thought,
Too deep to dig through.
　　Searching for a way to the other side.

YOUNG MAN

Tell me, young man,
   What intrigues your mind
      and twists it into a frenzy?
What draws you in closer?
Your soul is watching and waiting.

VINTAGE

Sweet and Tender.
    A desire to satisfy one of another.
Gently offering a touch that opens a path.
    Words of comfort,
Cradling looks of lust,
    Fulfilling a deep yearning
    Aged with time.

TASTE

The chance of change is
    At your fingertips.
An invitation to touch
      Your essence.
Awaken the deep, dark, desire
    Of your soul.

KNOWING

In that moment of time
    That leads to
    Opening a portal into the future.
Carrying with you what you yet do not know.
A guiding force that
    Connects you.
    Divides you.
    Changing everything.

TICK OF TIME

The exciting rush pushing on the urge of more to come.
The outpouring stuck behind a
    Trigger buried underneath
        Hope meets discovery.
The tick of time when
    It comes into the light,
Whether coerced or invited
    Perhaps purged from a knowing
    Or sliding out on it's own.
The next instance
    breaks ground,
    Leaving an opening,
A birth of the presence in the next new moment.
Unattached, exploring a new
    Place in time.

BRIDGE

Lucky are those that
      Stand on the bridge
    Waiting to cross.
Few are those who dared to step
    In the direction of the unknown.
Stillness comes when you
    Breathe in the sunshine.
For courage stands strong in the shadow,
    Grounded in the knowing.

ON HIGH

Exploring pleasure into the wee hours
    Of the morning.
      Surging again for another round of ecstasy.
Time collapses and expands beyond
    This world.
    When connections are made on high.

DRAMA

Drama, demise,
    Heartache, distain,
All because you feed on fear.
Fear of being seen, really seen.
    Shockingly enough, you are
    The only one that holds the key
    To unlocking the door of release.
Here you are,
    Waiting in the shadow
Filtering out all of who you really are.
Your true essence
    Marveling in the malicious.
Cut the reins. Reach out for Love.
For the world is waiting to be with you.
Shy and meek, so tender and sweet,
Helping to ease out the power of you.
Love's never-ending reaches beyond
    Your unforeseen limits.
Far past an endless
    Source or supply.

LESSONS OF LOVE

Lessons of love
First come from our mother's young.
So unfortunate for us,
To forget and then to remember what we are,
Designed from our
Father's Love.
Nothing deeper, nothing cleaner, nothing richer,
Nothing greater, than His Love.

State of Mind

Sit and wait, sending love.
    Building a fire of courage.
A window of time opens up
    With such a spark
The deep longing to be loved
    Hangs out on to the edge,
Hoping to catch the next wave
    Of experience.
A life preserver of sorts
    Thrown just at the right moment.
    Changing everything.

PORCUPINE

You push away with your snarl,
    Those that look your way.
Disdain fills your face as
    You prepare a path that
Only proves you are not worth their glance.
Laying the groundwork that no one can love you.
Anger rises up, ready for battle
To prove your unworthiness.
    Push comes to shove
As your armor grows spikes
    Like that of a porcupine.
Warding off even those that would
    Drop their dreams to help you down from a tree.
    You are scared.
Scared and alone.
Scared of the past and it's repeating future.
Scared of yourself and the pain
    That you feel.
Scared of seeing the truth.

SHAME

Shame
The "am" sits in the middle of Shame.
Making up a part of "me"
Uncovering and shedding away,
Finding what's hidden in between.
For it is a "she" and a "he"
Or just me?
Making something new, that was there since the Garden
of Eden.
Exposing.

Casting Call

The shell of a religion
    Becomes a cast.
Words bounce around off the outside
Echoing inside, the hollow interior.
Brilliant words of a new dimension
    Fall forward on the sterile ground.
For there is no possible route
    To any place new,
        Not even in the next season.
For Love has found a boundary,
    So small,
All it can do is
    To smother hope from all sides.

THE WAY OUT

Fear is like a piranha.
Chewing away at your ability to Love.
Stirring in the confusion of emotions
A black out occurs.

Stagnate, dark, without life.
Is this where you live?
Breathe deep into this desolate pit
    Of your own designed hell.
For it is the only way out.
        The only way to see Love
            On the other side.

THE ABYSS

The depths of Hell seem real
    When climbing down deep into who I am.
The part that has not learned Love.

CROW'S SONG

The caw of the crow
    Awakens the eyes of the soul.
Few see the depths and practice
    The patience of discovery.
A seeker seeks a searcher, a dreamer.
    Where tides rise and mountains move
    When the two meet.
Allowing the channel of the
    Spirit's essence to sing.

DEEP ROOTS

The retched pain of letting go
Realization so deep,
    Like none other.
The pain is more to God
When you are not in the light of
    His Love.
He mourns the passing of losing you
Giving you a choice
    To choose only His Love.

THE HOLY GRAIL

The time is now
    For you to set aside all that
    You hold between you and
Another one of God's perfect creation.
You lose in the end
    Without love.
For you will never taste God's Pure Light and Love
    Settle in, settle down.
        Drink from God's cup
And fill up.

TENSION

The ride
The fight
The right to be right
So strong it saturates
    More than one.
Changing possible futures
It's most frightening.
How to hold on, hold your ground,
When you think no one notices.
A quiet prayer releases the strength of Love
    From above.
Quenching all Hatred as if it never was.

RETCHED HOSPITALITY

A body holding on
    Tight with pain, full of might
Tension, Anger, Fear
    And more
Can have you take a different turn in
    All that you do.
How soon will you notice?
    It's desire to rest and refuge.
Listen, Learn, Love then Live.

LOST

Getting lost in nowhere
The somewhere of the moment,
Opens the unknown
    Seen by those who dare.
Live Richly, Jump out
Lean Forward
Tilt into the unknown.
Discover you!

STARK NIGHT

Stark night, Pure light
And all that is in between.
Swinging the pendulum
To and fro
Richly living your existence.

FREEDOM RINGS

My Love for you
  Is so tender and rich
Deep and endearing
Knowing all the time
  That I must let you go with each moment of time.
Letting you choose without a doubt,
This is where you want to be.
My longing to share all that I have is urgent
  It feels as though my heart will burst.
Navigating past my
  Own desires
  To love you even deeper.
Grateful for each memory
  Etched in my mind.
A reminder that I have loved without
Expectation defining only a one-sided relationship.
Sacrificing my own conditions
  As a gift for you to choose to
Love unconditionally.

TIME MACHINE

Time is a machine
Waiting on no one.
With each tick, it offers a choice
    And escapes unknowingly
    Like a vagrant in the night.

DARKNESS

Radiant, Brilliant, Sparkling Light.
    Glistening outwardly into the night.
Darkness bows on one knee
    Shielding its eyes from
        The Love that passes by.

CHOICE

Boxes and Boundaries
Guidelines and Rules
Designed to protect
   Each one from themselves.
In such a way it hinders growth
   Based on the silent but deadly
   Restriction of judgment.
Freedom of choice, your choice.
Choosing because of it,
   Or in spite of it?

WAKE UP

Listen to your soul screaming
   In pain, as the stab of the
   Cold, steel, blade repeats its
Strikes. Going deep into your heart.
Over and over
Look in the mirror.
Who holds the handle?

THE TRAIN STATION

Waiting expectantly for the moment
that will never come.
Why wait on the future?
Filled so, without a present present.
Moment to moment.
    Its moving on.
The train stops to let you off.
All is the now,
    For evermore.

THE WELL

Deep within
      Lies the secret place
That few discover.
Courage is your way to unravel
The place where you are the only guide.
Search until you find the untouchable spot.
      Breathe, Live, Light
A quiet ripple of your awakening
      Collides with the surface
      Releasing all of who you are
Making room to drink from
God's Well.
The one of perfect, pure light and love.

COCOON

A deep desire emerges to crawl up inside
      Of your soul,
             And sit still within.
Bringing in the power of Love.
Where no judgment can live.
Quietly breathing into the space that is you.
Lining the sides of your heart
      With truth and light.
Watering the tender, young growth
Of your essence yearning within.

THE ELEPHANT'S ROOM

As I sit and listen while colorful
    Melodies dance around my head,
I notice the quiet beating of a heart.
    Searching for its origin
I discover a gentle soul sitting next to me.
Unzipping the exterior, I climb ever
    so quietly inside,
For a chance to cradle your sweet and tender heart.
Nestled deep within the warmth
    I settle into its stillness
And feel the beat of life's drum.

ONCE AGAIN

In the moment that repeats itself
is a chance
To discover more.
Deeper inside
still you go
to release the spell that casts the shadow.
Thoughts linger, teetering on the edge of worry, hope,
doubt, and confusion...
Encompassing all of you
For this is like it was in the past,
Yet designed differently today
in hopes to release the troubled ego.

SLIPPING SIDEWAYS

When you find yourself once again in the place called
Hell. Where do you go from here?
Sitting still to discover there is no way out,
Or reaching past for places never visited
Because of blinded sight.

What happens in this moment?
Which defines your now and then.
Does it rectify the future
Or repeat the precious past?

Dipping into the unknown which seems so familiar can
last lifetimes,
But only if you care to remember.

WHY

Why is it?
The looking at the in between,
Knowing it is real.
Is it determined by the why and what?
And where from there do you go?
Who steals your thoughts, moments, and transgressions?
Let's be frank…
It's stealing only your time.
For when will you remember
Who brought you to this point?
Let the chips fall where they may
They will… Never… Forget…
And always remember.

BLACK HOLE

Pulling back towards an
Inward decline.
Forward movement within an
Encapsulating magnetism
Til a dead stop,
Inside a crevice.
A directional shift of fury recaps moments from the here
and now,
Yet measured against the chances of tomorrow.
Torture,
Torment, where such
Treacherous timing can
End in disaster.
When the knife slips against the potter's clay.
Shifting the force of harsh change,
Forming something ever so new.

A surprise awaits, within the eye of the beholder.

Timing, delay, manifestation,
Transition, malfunction of a malformation.

WINTER BEATS

Rain beats down on the fallen leaves of the trees,
While the sound of the morning train crescendos
approaching the nearby station.
The softened light of the day sets the scene of Winter.
Abiding in nature and nurture.
Married with chill in the air, inviting one to want to nestle down
into a place to rest.
Within the season of restoration and replenishment.
Searching for peace and comfort,
'Til Spring awakes with new hope.

Skeleton Self

Ever wonder whether you would find yourself,
Searching in the dark.
Hidden in the closet.
A skeleton you thought you'd never become.
Darker than night.
Yet flashes with a streak of light, shine bright.

Where did it come from?
How did it get here?
Why do I become what I did not know?

Pain, intrigue, disguised in the night.
Clanging calamities causing confusion and fright.
Darkness versus light.

Such difference, in a day when reflected against the
night.
How did I become what I never thought I might?

SILENCE

Deafening.
Confining.
Exacerbating.
Defining.

Ridiculous when playing childlike roles.

Can you speak?
If so, if in love and then play in truth?

Or shall you remain a dictator. Confused and deceptive.

THE KNIGHT

He is the master
He is the King.

He is the one

Who controls everything.

The this, and the that

And of course, which ever presently defines
The light.

That which is called the night.

This way
That way

Searching, as if
He's stumbling over his own might.

SEARCHING

What are you looking for…
A penny,
A thought,
A memory,
Or recognition.
Perhaps it's understanding.

Looking within the spaces of the dark trenches of the
sidewalk
Or between the lines of the poem,
script,
or movie?

What are you searching for?

What do you hope for?

What will you find?

The answer?
Or, another question?

STANDING THERE

Standing there, frozen in time.
     The race of my heart
          Begins.
Wonderment, intrigue.
The thrill
Of past memories
     Exploring the surge.
How fast it takes me there
     Magnifying
My future thoughts.

LAPS

Waves begin and laps caress. Shimmering within the light.
Moving past the shore that changes.
And midnight that starts half-there's and here's, and downs
and ups again.
When and where?
Who will decide?
Whether starlight dances on the tops or hides in between?
Wondering what shall be next. Along the river... Who will
decide,
The locks behind?
Lock boxes of crevices. Many moons, of a shining moon.
There's more to discover, amongst the shallows of the shore.
Shall it be here, there,
Or somewhere in between while the water waits.
For some.
Thing.
No.
More.

UNDER IT ALL

In the dark and dreary closet,
    Under a blanket of dust.
You find the lonely place,
When you are searching for the lost coin out of your
pocket.
A button that's fallen astray.
Within the dark recesses is where you will uncover
secrets from the past,
    Lived long ago and
    Hidden from the light.
Waiting to die without notice.

FLAVORED MIX

Sweet and spicy
    Flavored in the mix.
Varietal intellect seasoned with feelings of another
    Outside myself.
For gratitude and grace are sent with love.
    Do I let myself dip into what is next?
Far away, reaching in, when I'm in between
    What is me.
Why contemplate the future? For all I have is now.
Being loved by me.

SEASONS

Seasons come and seasons go.
    All while wondering if it might snow.
So much impossibility every second
    Floats by,
When thinking it's something
You can control.
A storm may come, or you might go,
    Sometimes even wondering if there could ever be
        A breeze to cool the day's heat.
And then again, how often do you
    Even notice,
    What time the sunsets?
        The last time it rained?
Taking time to notice the moment
    Under the stillness you find within.
There is a wonderment as to why I question
    The meaning or purpose of
    How I spend my days.
Offering up to my sweet soul, the room, and possibility
    To breathe and remember.
That my existence of a lifetime is built on every moment
in between.

Deep Within

The view deep within your eyes
Exists far beyond what this world holds.
Your tender touch sneaks past the watchful guard of a
healing heart.
Offering a chance to view what most never see.
Your expressed depth of love lives past the gentle words you
share.
Its fragrant, magnetic mysticism awakens the seed of
searching souls.
Rich treasures of redemption are reconciled, as gratitude
kneels at its feet.

DEFINING MOMENT

Up and down, to and fro,
   everywhere and all around.
Episodes dance in the light of day
  Until the night is here to stay.
Definitions of who I am
   Float deep within the swirl.
Spinning the cause and effect
  Of escalading shadows,
And spotlighting disaster
with no hope in sight.
  Tortured thoughts
  Creep deep into my dreams.
While a bitter taste of what is to come
   Scorches my tender palate.
Tethered from one day to the next.
The moment searches for an early morning dew,
   To quench
   The ache
     Of the latest chapter.

BRICKS AND MORTAR

Pain,
Dismay,
Disrupt,
And dismantle.
Shaking the cornerstones of the foundation.
Each chance brings in something new.
A choice to stand strong,
Or to watch it crumble down around you.

Do you rise above the rubble?
Or fall to your knees?
Ever hope that your dreams can define the steadiness of the
rocky structure?

Where do you turn?

When will the cycle of madness ever end?

PEOPLE

Percolating pots of perception.
Porous and cantankerous.
Promising, yet polluting of
Mind, body, and soul.
Perfection propagates from sensible to disturbing,
Forthright and Loving,
Intentional and Caring.
Subjective for sure.
Surprisingly susceptible
To Love and the essence of Fear.
Hold out, at each moment
For the choice is clear.

Buying Time

Positioned within alleys of uncertainty.
Yet, aligned in between the
    Streets of Desire.

Where does one run when all eyes
    Are watching?
Amid the hope of going unnoticed
    In a world of here and now.
Life skips chapters, while the heart
    Misses a beat, fighting through
    The confusion.

Nervousness shrinks in the shadows
    Of the nearby streetlamp.
Pondering anxiety and
    Pleasure amongst a bed of riches.

WAITING

Waiting, waiting in the moment of
Waiting.
An impasse as it seems.
Breathe normally and exhale.
Letting it go.
Making a clearing.
    Opening new paths to your heart.
Tough for some
    As they will never make the journey.
Even tougher for those that do.

Spring

SPIRITS LOVE

Spirit of my soul
Deep, dark, desire
My greatest lover of me.
    Surrounding myself with
Love's pure light.
    So rich, it's hard to take in.

METAMORPHOSIS

He reaches through her
    Past every known, landing on who she is.
Breathlessness has overcome her
As she waits
To see her lover in the flesh.
All that he is and all that is
    To be awakened.
That night is to come
    Where there is no separation.
The night where fire redefines expectation.
Transforming light into love.

YOUR LIGHT

Is it hidden underneath Greed and Jealousy?
Tainted by Hatred and Anger?
    Quite a disservice to your fellow man
    And to yourself.
We all notice in one way or another
    By your words or actions.
Wise words of a loving legacy say,
    Bring your light out on the stand
        So others can see
That darkness cannot stay.

THIS OR THAT

The spot in time where new possibilities begin.
                    So precious,
        Like a new blade of grass.
It struggles to sprout and grow in the newness of light,
        Tender to the touch.
Shaped by its hopeful surroundings.

Faithful Fear waits in the corner
        To rear its ugly head,
Destroying this new life
        One thought at a time.

LOTTERY

Deep, dark, hidden pain
    Covered in years of despair
Suffocating the life beneath.
One moment of time appears, when chance enters, rolling
the dice for love to preside.
Governing the possibility of a new
    Existence for this
        Tender soul to live.

PATH

Taste the tantalizing tinkle of truth.
    Let it whisper a challenge to your heart's desire
Bringing you a chance of a lifetime.
Enabling you just a moment where life changes forever.
Exposing a new path
To the young brave explorer.

THE EYES HAVE IT

The eyes hide nothing.
    Not the dread of the past, nor the hope of the future.
Not the pain of remembrance or the strain of hope.
Hard to conjure up the
    Wishes of childhood,
Distinguished as Candyland dreams
    And rainbow fantasies.
But now and again
    A flicker appears
        As quick as a spark.
    That promotes a glimmer of difference
Between what was and what will be.

AWAKEN

Much to do, to see, to discover
Uncover and awaken.
Reaching in, past everything.
Raw to the touch.
Present to the smell of
An existence not yet realized.
And discovering the taste
For the very first time.

WHOLENESS

Swirling colors so brilliant and bright
    Cascading into a web
        Of iridescent waves.
Parts of a whole, not complete without another.
Surround yourself in the light.
Swim in its waves beyond all that you know.
Realizing you are a part of the whole.

THE NEST

Quiet solitude, a resting place.
    A chance to breathe
        And create a space.
Where dreams are made and wishes granted.
Hearts unfold and the
    Mind opens.
Letting in the everlasting invitation
To settle down and nestle in.
In the place you call home.

FORMATION

The taste of something new starts in a thought.
Only the sensation of the experience
    Can be handled when in formation.
Provoking thoughts, raising ideas and
    Growing in desire,
Feeding a hungry soul.
Tasting Life like never before,
    Over and over
Beginning another cycle of discovery.

WONDERMENT

Share with me what is in your heart.
What is waiting to be heard?
Your mind is entertained with
    Too many thoughts not shaped
        By reality.
You create a riddle with no
    Available answer.
All to keep you locked away.
Where you think you are protected.

KALEIDOSCOPE

Floating in colors mesmerized by
    Much of nothing.
Faceted matrices
    Fashioned much like a prism's reflection of light.
Shifting and changing as each breath
    Escapes.
Heart chakra green surrounded
    By Love's pink light.
Surviving in a kaleidoscope
    With no end in sight.

SNAILS, SPIDERS AND THE LIKE

Snails, spiders and ants of all sizes.
    Roaming the newly rained on ground.
How freeing to an ant,
Off on his next adventure
Not held back by his past.

Green Room

Step inside the green room,
    Where all fades away.
The spotlight of eternal Love
    Is the only light
Breaking free of the darkness,
In a brilliant sort of way.

LIGHT FALLS (WATERFALL)

Climbing high and bringing down
 A chance of light.
The bridge to the soul
 Where all are one.
Swim deep, dig in
 Soak up the rays of God's Love
For it is the great I Am for all.

MEET UP

Resting and waiting, while knowing
    What is next.
Movement, clarity for the moment,
Defined as crossing paths for the 1000th time.
Yet, meeting for the very first time.

INVITATION

Wanting to jump into your world,
> Capturing your movements and thoughts.

Enveloping you in my mind to create a new way to know.
> The separate part that is me wishes

The difference in an invitation.
Perhaps, a kidnapping of sorts.
Capturing all that you are.
All the same, wanting to have the best of both worlds.
While honoring a space for the creation of this adventure.
Discover how love fits best between you and me.

LOVE, SWEET LOVE

Gratitude, Grateful, Thankfulness.
  Words too small to define.
The Grace of being Loved.
A deep, place opens.
  Clearing the dusty parts away.
Shining Light on Both.
You can feel the Love
    When you aren't looking for it, expecting it,
    Even from the most unsuspecting places.
Opening up you. Opens up them, unknowingly.
A feeling or sense is there,
    That it could be possible.
    Just for a moment
        To taste Love, Sweet Love
It is a gift that needs no acknowledgement.
    Gratefulness is Humbling
    To those who can taste it.

YOUR LOVE

Opens up a space for me,
    To be.
I feel no limits to my ability.
The restrictions that life gives us all
    Just to make me small.
      Being in the moment of
Pure Love, it's judgment free,
    With an open invitation.

MAP

Direction, purpose,
    Guidance, path.
Reverence for what you do not know.
Make room to hear the voice from above.
Always knowing.
Always loving.

FRESH

Letting go in all
    Your things
    Your thoughts
Your boundaries
Your hopes and dreams
Bringing in Love and Truth
Light the way for so many and yourself.
Looking deep into the mirror
Recognize the God, given truth
Of Love, Sweet, Love.

BLESSED

Leaves, Trees, Forests, Regions.
The part of the whole
Which is the all or sum.
Derived from the parts of the whole.
Defined as
Limits or infinity
Rich, poor
Sick, healed
Small, large
Empty or complete.
Imprisoned or blessed.
Searching to fleeing.

EYEING IT

Deep within your eyes, in your path of knowing,
Colored by your understanding.
Traveling the path within
Dissolves away your earthly look
    Leaving only your legacy for view.
Lifetimes of definitions are carried away as the work begins.
Unraveling all that envelops around the
    Treasure called Love.

THE FISHERMAN

Angry healers can plant a seed
    Of Betrayal.
    Like a freshly baited hook
To catch a fish.
You drag the line
    Battling the choice
    For yourself.

Bite down hard.
Taste the offer
Make a choice, to let it go
    Or to swallow it whole.

MEADOW

Now, is still and quiet
No attachment
Clean
Beautiful and effervescent
A space, a clearing
Room to Breathe in
Like the meadow I visit on High.

SURRENDERING INTO SPRING

A soft breeze whispers among the branches,
Creating the tantalizing tingle of the wind chime
Floating a melody into the evening air.

Springtime hints at her start, moving through
    The fresh green sprigs of grass.
Quietly gathering momentum to burst
Out new growth.
Bringing the pitter patter of rain to the sidewalk.

BEAUTY AND THE BEHOLDER

A paradox of sorts.
Where Beauty lies and the owner decides.
Who holds it?
All forms,
Deep within
    Or riding on the outside.
Who is the judge and gets to decide?
Beholding such a treasure....
    Does it require an admirer?

LIVING

When it comes, bringing questions, answers,
    Thoughts, and provocations.
Feeling of a high and a
    Disastrous low.
All while waiting for the next moment of what
    You thought was going to happen.
    Or are you really living?
        Perhaps you're wishing?
Wishing yourself away, all that there isn't.

A GIFT

In this world, not of this world.
    No boundaries or judgments here.
Just me, myself and what I give.
Share the journey with me.
Give me a moment to
    Show you how much
        You matter.
How much you are loved
In God's perfect light.

LOTUS BLOSSOM

Potential awaits within,
 Underneath the outer layers.
Petals stiff and weathered surround the outside
 Holding the blossom together.
Layer after layer unfolds to something new,
 Just as each day starts with the morning sun.
Revealing a fresh, brilliant
 Source of wonderment
As soft petals rich in fragrance unveil
 The tender source of beauty inside.
Unlike anything ever seen before.

Mental Notes

Spirit, help me see where I can speak
    About what I need,
    to be gentle,
And lovingly hold out only the truth for me,
    Others.

YOU ARE

You are my Love, the Beloved.
    Full and Complete.
Breathe in the nourishing fruit of God's Touch.
Surrender to the sacred goodness
    Bestowed especially for you.
You are Beloved, my Love.

FIELDS OF BLOOM

Where are you now?
    Living forward in the future?
Dragging the past so heavy behind you?
While expectancy trembles
    Only to be forgotten in the present.
Where are you now?
A place of reflection,
    One of wonder.
Where seeds are planted
    And fields blossom
Over a season of time.
Offering a reflection
    Of decisions past,
Flowing freely like a wave of wheat
Blowing in the wind.
Dreams blossom, while
    Discontent is nurtured.
And the reap of a Summer's harvest,
Offers hope to an aging farmer.

MELODY

Wandering through the notes,
Floating on the next measure.
Dreams that realized and yet hopes only mesmerized,
for the life that is not yet seen.
Questions escape where wonderment is felt, while all moments
blend.
When people sing on the plains of ancestors,
Marching with bells that did ring.
It remains to be seen.

What wonder could this life bring?
In the waiting for the measure, in between.

SHIFT IN FOCUS

Twists and turns through delight and misunderstanding
happens,
When life brings you the moments out of focus.
For what was, is not to be within the acknowledgment
of the concrete present.
Happiness and freedom tow the party line.
Where you stand, is where you will be judged.
Darkness and Delight are our partners that no one
would ever presume.
Only question when out of focus.

HIGH NOON

High noon, where two hands meet

And many gather,
After wandering through the morning.

A gentle gesture of love...
And life,
Join together
In it's highest good.

Celebrating a new union.

Your love,
courage,
hope
and discovery
engulf me into wanting more.

More of a lifetime of passion,
desire,
And rich blessings.

I will honor you
Support you,
Love you,
And hold you close to me
For the rest of my days.

And as I steal a line from our favorite movie,
Would that be all right with you?

RAIN

In the middle of Hell,
let there be rain,
to quench the loss
and fuel the love.
Where desire raises its head
and leaps into
what's next.
Where life is lived,
and Grace is found.

Let there be Rain.

MUD PUDDLES

Just after a storm
When the rain has gone,
There is a freshness in the air.
The crisp scent of something new
    Lingers, electrifying your senses.
Puddles of rain
    Gathered on the top of the Earth
    Seep gently in when nurtured
    By a farmer's tending.
For on untended ground, puddles
    Form and wait.
Lingering out in the open, easy to see.
    Shining bright in the sun's reflection.
Mud rises up when people pass by.
    Carrying the weight of their load.
Unable to loosen the mud stuck
    Between their toes.
This ground is not
    Fertilized from the tender care of a watchful eye.
Rather, it's like a trap.
    Those that walk by, leave tracks
Leading back to the mud puddle of my pain.
Take time to sit in the storm.

To be washed by the rain.
Cleansing the depths of your soul
    And nurturing the soil.
I sit and wait until the grey sky
    Becomes crystal blue.
And the smell of new life
    Overwhelms my senses.
Open your eyes to a brand-new day.

SPRING

As bright and fresh as a young child.
Wondering into Easter morning.

Awakening to what is next,
Surprise, delight, wonderment.
Sometimes more than the mind can hold.

Love waiting
Joy exuding, unlike a sneeze exploding in the moment.
Expectant happiness raining down as bright as the day's sun.
A day full of laughter and so
Much
Fun
Leaves one exhausted from the day,
A nap awaits.
And dreams begin.

Summer

GOLDEN NUGGET

A tasting of sorts of the highest regard.
    A banquet feast offered as a nugget of Truth.
Each bite of this Truth reveals more of my heart,
    The opening that can follow when each morsel is
swallowed,
        Then digested.
    Nourishing my tender soul.

COLLISION

Tentacles reaching forward.
Then, drawing back
   Within its reach,
Craving the effervescence of what is to come.
The waves stand still, storing its potential,
   Awaiting the burst of kinetic release into the next moment.
The moment where truth and love, collide.
And, come crashing in.

THE DINER

Convoluted confusion,
Cultivating the unknown.
Stirred together with the wand of illusion.
Seared with things from the past.
The taste, burns the tongue so tender to the touch,
Yet seems paired so sweetly with the night's daily special.
Curious which patrons will partake.

POWER

Birds on a wire.
    Gathering in numbers.
Resting or waiting for the perfect moment of flight
Never thinking of the charge beneath their feet.
Oblivious to the power flowing at the speed of light.

TIDAL WAVE

The moment of truth,
    Plain as the day.
So strong nothing else can hold on.
Opening up every crevice
    That needs it.
Drink in the light.
Feel the burn,
    Seeping into your abyss.
For a ripple has started.
    The tide is coming.
Bringing waves of reflection through your soul.

BASKET WEAVE

The lines of a basket
   Appear as weaves in time.
Pathways cross and journeys collide.
Traveling around not knowing the difference
   Between the beginning and the end.
Waiting for the next turn or junction
   Of space in between, now and then.

THE LINES OF A WEAVE

Weaves of time.
Pathways cross and journeys collide.
It's movement travels around,
    Not knowing the difference
        Between the beginning
        And the end.
Waiting for the next turn, under, over or for the in
between.
Dependent of the clock, the tick between the tock.

MESSAGING

Colors all around,
Messages sent and received; green, blue, red, and yellow.
All unique in its own light.
Working together to color the day.
Joining as one and separate,
    Yet the same.

THE ROAD

Where do you go, when you go?
When you do not know?
Back to the same?
Expecting something different?
Sounds of crazy sing high in the trees.
All things are yet the same.
And always will be.
Choose to continue, on the path that binds.
Etching a deeper rut.
Fooling those following in behind you.
Consistency is safe and guarded,
Never changing shape or form.
Never creating anything not already seen.

Cure

Tantalizing desire teases every nerve ending,
    Creating a twinge
        Of un-comfortableness.
Knowing safety simmers seasonally, for the fire can burn.
    Yet the continuous years of searching agitates
        Your nervous twitch.
All while waiting for a cure,
    From the next connection.

THIRSTY ROAD

A remembrance of your path
    From long ago.
A knowing so rooted to your core.
Dip into the pool of light.
    Taste the effervescent of the
    Water of life.
Drink until you are no longer
    Thirsty.
Till all your desires
    Have been met.
This is just for you and always has been.
To taste your goodness and might.

LIFE WITHOUT LIFE

The happenstance of existence, where there is
   No living.
A death in life. Torturous.
    Only a few discover
      A way out
Of this everyday life, a life with a life.
One with living.
    Awake, alive, so full of a
True Existence.

LINGER

Movement, a tingle from within
    Just under the skin.
    Enough to remain unsettled,
In a instance.
    Lasting momentarily, only for a minute.
Unfed, this craving rises up.
Begging one to ask the question.
    How is it that you can't
    Sit still?
Lingering in the shadow
    Of the last waking thought.
Like a small child, hidden round the corner
Covering her snicker,
Hoping to remain unseen.

MIRROR

A mirror speaks softly in one's sight.
Seemingly sequestered
    By its maker,
The researcher or the critic.
You know because you've seen it.
A looking glass of reflection
Showing yourself in the raw.
Beauty or Judge,
    Who decides the right?
Look beyond your silvered borders
Fragile against any stone.
You see and You know
    The truth beyond Your will to be right.

DRY GROUND

Out in the woods,
    Sitting.
Drenched in sunlight
    Hitting the ground like a spotlight,
    Deep between the trees.
Sadness spills out,
As the feeling of warmth
    On my skin begins to burn.
Sadness of a time before, such singing sadness,
    Still hanging on.
The anguish of the ache.
Where is my solitude?
    When I only find myself
Swimming in my own tears, while on dry ground.

DAY DREAMING

Spirit, what is in it for me
    To know?
What are my dreams you tell me,
    In the light of day?
Restless, deep sleep, watching for
    The story to unfold.
Grasping at a glimpse of my reality.

MEN

Men,
From the world of the Unknown.
So many are far beyond a place
Of connection, to anyone
But themselves.
Shaped by the women so boldly
Branded their stay on his skin.
Torture and torment last long after
A moment.
Far longer than Love can hold on.

INTO THE LIGHT

Tell me about your sadness,
     That which keeps you cocooned.
    This sadness that you try on.
Honoring every piece by tasting it with all of
     Your senses.
    Fashioning a change on high.
For it is heaven when such delight is created,
    And brought into the light.

VACATION

Escaping back into the pain
     Of the past.
    Lounging there as if on vacation
    From the present.
While your storm rages inside
     Life travels to the next
    Moment in time.
    You'll miss your essence.
Seasons of pain and sadness.
      Some covered in an illusion
      Of self-medication.
    Drama, drinking, drugs and denial
For it is not your reality, but
    An excuse to hide,
      To be inside.
Where safety is only a
    Deception.

VESSELS

What you feel is what you are.
An open vessel full of Earth's
      Richest treasures.
    What you are, you feel.
No questions surrounding your
   Unknown.
For you can only see what
   Is known.
Try it all on for yourself, this
Love that you say is so
   Tender and sweet.
You are what you feel about the other.
The presence offered as a mirror
The present offered as a present.

NAKED AND FAMOUS

Showing up
    Creating a space
        Surrounded by mayhem.
Stillness sets in
    For all to see and feel
        Play with and try on.
Methods or madness
    Unleashing the power
    From the heavens.
Why no one notices
    Is of no fault of their own.
Just a chance for the queen to love.
    Love from on high.
    Giving away just enough
To taste.

BEETLE DREAMS

Blessings and desires
　　Fill the night,
Dripping into dreams
　　Lush and beautiful,
　　Like the Egyptian beetle
Sparkling with the rainbow's color.
Playfully buzzing
　　And dancing in the sunlight.
Bringing news of riches,
　　More wondrous than Christmas morning.
Hold on and sit still
　　For there are many more things to come.

IN THE DISTANCE

Every moment brings me back to you.
A thought, a word, a passing memory.
Wherever you are not, I am searching.
Wishing for the next moment to arrive,
    Right beside me.
Desire and wishes hang within reach
    Just within sight.
Yet, not able to grasp ahold.
    The longing, seeps up from the shadows
Forming an image to be seen
Only from a distance.
The ache of wanting you near,
Bubbles up with effervescence,
    Just like the new day's sun rising.

ONE NIGHT IN BANGKOK

Deep within the night she lays asleep,
Drenched in passion's light.
Soaked with the night's fulfillment of desire,
And exhausted by Love's sweet song.

Yet still, she finds herself waiting in between the lines of a stanza.
Simply for the measure to sound the next note.
Wondering where righteousness can be found.

Evermore, discovering each new composition
And the difference from the next.

Continually riding the vibrations outward,
Stretched out on the sound of Hope.

THE SUIT

Injustice, righteousness
    Are the threads that hold judgment
        Together.
The seamstress of limitation allows more of the same.
Binding the hope that is to be.
    Treacherous, brittle, breakable,
Sewn in the in-between.

SUNRISE

The morning begins slowly awakening from
A night's slumber.
Rising up to meet the day.
Cascading Light into the farthest corner.

SUNBATHING

Unexpected gifts
    Of all shapes and sizes
Are unwrapped when Love is present.
Life's lessons are a blessing.
    A gift meant only for you.
Embrace your essence.
      Uncover your truth.
        Bask in the Light of Love.

BATTLE LINES

Raging thoughts of passion
    Beside the quiet space of honor.
Struggling with the inviting
    And the capturing of your every move.
Disastrous danger lies across
    The line of definition and boundary.
Love spreads her wings of grace,
    Casting a shadow
    For all who dare to camp at the frontlines of Romance.

TSUNAMI

Settling in on top of the Tsunami.
    Battling the urge to fall into the wave
Or to sit quietly on top and silently watch the storm,
As it rages beneath.
    Tasting the choice with your toes.

A WALKABOUT

A journey beyond your limits
    Of understanding
Spending all that you are
On losing yourself.
All to discover the Light
    After a new awakening.
May you choose the path that is
    Shrouded in courage.
      For there is nothing that compares.

OUTSIDE

Together,
Riding the waves
     Of where to go.
My side kick at my side.
     We set off to
          Explore the unknown.

HUNGER

Riches beyond the Human Element
A transition happens.
    Brilliant, enlightened
Few can reach the infinitesimal existence.
Quiet, no thoughts
    Overwhelming Love.
Human emotions need cleaning out
    In order to reach in
      And taste all
    God has to offer.
Bright, Pure, White, Light
    So juicy.
      It feeds all Hunger.

DEFINITION

Your definition of Love will be Challenged.
Your ability to know, to show...
Being scared of knowing who you are
     And how to love,
          Serves no one.
WAKE UP! For you are being called to be all!

FAR AWAY

Far away, yet right at home.
The peace that follows
      When you know
            You are loved.
Full breath of Love
      Followed by light
Take this with you wherever you go.

SURREAL

Leave everything
   Leave your home, your house.
Leave all that you know.
Expect nothing in exchange for everything
Making room for all that you are to grow.

THE POOL

Swimming head
    Swirling thoughts.
Taking you away from your knowing of
Rage that follows confusion.
When you dare not see
 The precious clearing of what is not,
    For you to hold.

TRAVEL

The possibility of surviving the journey
Through the eye of the needle
Is your mind's question which
Stops you dead in your tracks.
The thought of the preposterous processing
Presenting its pain is particularly paralyzing.
Until you try, how will you know…
That the persnickety persistence
Of your heart can propel you past all there is.
Revealing only Your Truth.

CROUCHING TIGER

Crouched into the corner.
    Claws drawn for the attack.
The smell of Fear hangs thick in the air.
For it knows it has been found
And can disappear without a trace, deep within the night.
The tiger of mindful self will die
    A slow painful death.
Hanging on to every last thread of hope
    Until
It is needed no more.

TRUTH

Sharp, freeing
Deafening, exhilarating
Painful
Discreet
Abstract and Concrete.
Spoken in the weight of a scale,
The timing of crossing the finish line,
A man standing in front of a tank in Tiananmen square,
The etching on a cold tombstone.
Defining yet another moment of your reality.

The truth is better heard....
    When severed from the tether of judgment.

BLUE SKY

Sky blue,
    The brilliance of clarity,
    Reining above our heads.
Decorated with the contrasting white of puffy clouds
    The water of life.
Drifting free
    Of shape and from form.

YOUR EYES

Deep within your eyes, in your path of knowing,
Colored by your understanding.
Traveling the path within
Dissolves away your earthly look
    Leaving only your legacy for view.
Lifetimes of definitions are carried away as the work begins.
Unraveling all that wraps around the
    Treasure called Love.

LIFETIMES

Days come and go.
    Nights of transition follow.
I am here only to Love,
      Only to Love.
    Let transgressions approach.
Then, fall like the bullets in front of Neo.
Nothing can take me from my
    Father's Love.

DARK CREVICES

From the crusted crevices
    Warming up to heated lava.
Oozing from the depths of darkness,
In hopes of finding light
    To explode into.
Too close and you will get burned,
    And start your own path of pain.

THE WAY OUT

Fear is like a piranha.
    Chewing away at your ability to Love
Stirring in the confusion of emotions.
A black out occurs.
    Stagnate, dark, dead.
Is this where you live?
Breathe deep into the desolate pit.
    Of your own designated hell.
For it is the only way out.
    The only way to see Love
        On the other side.

LOSE YOURSELF

Lose yourself
    Of all that seems familiar, to
Pry away your judgment.
    Limiting your ability to see.
Look for the first time, where you stand
    In your own way.
In the way of the Truth.

DEEP DARK DISASTER

Old, dark, deep pain resides in the depths
    Infecting the future.
Wise up, Dear One.
    Let it serve you with experience.

UNKNOWING

Pain so deep,
    Beyond all I've known.
The gift is in where it takes me.

FOXHOLE

Confusion, pain,
Sinking further into a foxhole.
Ready for battle known only to my soul.
Spirit awakens your attention.
Seething disdain,
    That bumps into others.
Dark and alone with only
    One way out.
Look up.
    See the light.
Call to it.
Let it answer. Listen.

FRACTURED

The searing scorch
    Of cleansing clarity,
Burning beyond recognition.
Movement begins like Lava on freshly broken ground,
Lying deep within the crucible.

SPIRIT'S LOVE

Spirit of my soul
Deep, dark, desire
My greatest lover of me.
      Surrounding myself with
Love's pure light
      So rich it's hard to take in.

RELEASE

Tantalizing desire
    Hangs in the air.
      Building moment to moment
    Of one thought
    Shifting into a feeling,
    Followed by a hope of a night to come.
Leaving passion and persistence to stumble into her day.
Capturing her thoughts
    Like a thief in the night.
Awaiting the release of her lover's touch.

TWILIGHT DANCING

Disastrous desire reigns havoc deep within.
Etching a path of discovery down an uncharted road.
Searching unknowingly for any subtle gestures round every bend.
While cautious curiosity dances under the twinkle of each night's
twilight.
Persuasively, prevailing Love's Hope pushes forward,
Navigating through something new.

HEART SENSE

Where you are and where you desire....
Is only one wink away
From knowing within, that
Deep beyond where You thought ever existed,
Is a space.
Consider for a moment, that You are ... All and More.
Therefore,
When there is a yearning
Of Your heart,
Don't beat around.
Step in. Let Love abound.

OCEANS INSIDE

Diving deep
   Into a delicious taste, breaks new ground.
Somewhere inside
The Master awakes,
   Craving the next level of many seas.
Questions collide
   Where answers are known,
Within the wave of many desires.

EFFERVESCENT

Dripping wet,
Sparkly and bubbly,
The effervescence of love dances and sings as sweetly as spring rain.

Tossing and turning to define its existence. Amidst the sea and salty air.
Patience is key, to see it through.
A keen eyesight foretells of safe navigation to the surface for a breath of Love.

DISTRACTIONS

Distractions of the day,
Stir the crazy
Floating in my head.
Keeping me held captive.
Daily work clears my path,
Where Love can filter in.
Moment by moment,
Freeing me in it's stillness.
Precious is the day where this is all I do.

Oceans of Fruit

There it is.
The wide-open space,
  An ocean of endless possibilities.
No invitation is necessary,
  For the mist of the crashing waves
Draws you in, as it lands on your
  Outstretched toes.
Not even curiosity belongs on the shoreline.
It would be considered a foreigner.
This is the land that knows no stranger.
  Comfort, solitude, and a gentle nature
  Are planted in the garden beyond the gate.
The only discovery is to taste the fruits of each passing season.
Bountiful even in a record-breaking year.

NAVAL DIVING

The emptiness
of the deep, dark, hole,
Is vast.
When one swims amongst
themselves.
Not even aware they are absorbed within the well.
Perpetual dark disaster awaits one who suffocates in their own
presence.
Will they ever decide there's a moment of truth?
To breathe?
To look up?
Or to even pause,
For something new?

MOMENT IN TIME

Judgment in a moment of time
    Changes everything.
It defines what is and what will be.
It's calculated the same
    As when you measure your current state of mind.
There is no going back.

UNTITLED

The stuff called life that lives in me
Creates confusion when out of focus.
Stumbling towards the dark, searching to try and find its way.
     Staggering to what feels like falling into enlightenment.
Each new day affords the luxury
Of discovering lost traits,
     of rich treasures, yet to be discovered
Stepping out of darkness and into the light.

CLOUDS

White and puffy, posing here and there, in the sky above
    Frolicking like a child in the park.
Mystical Magi's of shape and form, alluding to its viewer's eye.
Hills and valleys, mountains and oceans; forming shapes of all kinds
within every moment.
    As vast as our imagination and as gentle as your lover's most
tantalizing touch.
These floating masses cause us to confuse reality with illusion.
    To search for reasons why it possibly could not really be.
Such things as a baffling conundrum caused from the jolts on an airplane
flight,
    Flying thru the imaginary wall.
To viewing the masquerade of the most peaceful sunset even while in
turmoil.
Clouds, thick or thin.
    Clouds, white as light or as dark as night.
        So many possibilities.

LOVE

Abandon the hurry,
Settle into the calm depths of your heart.
Removing the way you see.
Listen from that place.
The place where worlds collide
And boundaries disappear.
Releasing all that you are
And melting into all that there is.

ACKNOWLEDGMENTS

My heartfelt appreciation goes to my talented husband, Dr. Lee Chilton, for your innate ability to heal our community in such a troubled time and for doting over my poems early on in our relationship. I value this and your continued support throughout the formation of this book beyond what words can express. The poem "BECAUSE" is written to express my gratitude for all that you do for so many.

I'm eternally indebted to my children, Jake and Rusty, for their zest for life. Every day you both teach me so much about myself as well as about this world. Thank you. My deepest gratitude belongs to my lifelong best friend, Denise LaManna, and her family: my goddaughter Gabby, Luke, and Michael. Thank you for your love and support over so many decades.

My friends Matt and Karen Manroe, Kristie Kelly, Phil and Rita Barousse, Kathryn Weldon, and Kimberly Mills have stood by me and supported me over the years, providing love and guidance in countless ways. Patty Mendoza Lefner offered her endearing friendship and gets credit for my great photo, taken one fall day in Austin. You all encourage me to find hope in my tomorrows.

Having a deep desire to express myself through poems and turn it into a book is as hard as it seems. The adventure has been challenging, rewarding, and fulfilling, to say the least. With that, I thank my publisher, Cynthia Stone at Treaty Oak Publishers, for taking a chance on me and for holding my hand during the process.

Also my gratitude goes to Dr. Evelyn Robertson for her ability to masterfully edit in a heartbeat.

Thanks also go to my contributors and friends for your support and endearing commentaries: Kathryn Kershner Weldon, Alistair D., Mark

Dickens, and Phil Barousse.

Lastly, to anyone who has read my poems and to those who will read them: May you take what you like and leave the rest. Kudos to you for stepping in, even for a minute, and trying on a different point of view.

For this, may you be *Blessed Beyond Your Belief* in your journey.

NOTE FROM THE AUTHOR

Looking back, I never liked English class and the interpretation of poems - or any literature for that matter. It didn't seem to make much sense. I was horrible at it. Just ask my English teacher, who is still my friend today.

At the end of my first marriage, I was grieving the loss of my world as a stay-at-home mom for 16 years. Every part of my life was turning upside down. I walked, meditated, drew, cried, and screamed long into the night, just enough to be able to breathe. My family was being ripped apart. My reality was walking away into the middle of the night. Never to be seen again. It was heartwrenching. I knew if I did nothing, I would lose myself. I later wrote a poem about this time called *Surrender*.

My poems are influenced by the ancient Persian greats, Rumi and Hafez, whose writings I happened upon during a meditative weekend retreat. Their love of nature, the human spirit, and inner human turmoil lit a fire in me. One night after meeting a young lover I sat down to write. *The Night Collection* was born. And so was my love of writing short poems. When reading this collection, you will see that two of of these poems mirror one another. First reading *Anticipation* and then *Desire* reflects the same scene from two different perspectives. I was imagining my young lover, standing outside my front door with torrid visions floating in his head. While I, on the other side, felt my heart racing as I approached the door to let him in. Ahhh, *Anticipation* and *Desire*!

You could say my writing has become a form of therapy. Now it is clear to me what Poetry is: an art form of human expression. A translation of our human experience throughout life's seasons. It can be seen as either dark and cold or breath-taking goodness and light. That decision is left up to the interpreter and their lens. With that as my guide to living the experience of what I call my life, I have written over 300 poems in hopes to get them published. That day has come.

For now, that is my story, and these are my poems – so far. I am a lover of people. Passionately expressive. Fascinated by our nature, the human spirit, and how it translates into what we call life, I remain inspired. This will never change.

Made in the USA
Coppell, TX
01 April 2022

75881861R10118